THE AUTHOR'S PLATFORM:
WHAT IT IS
AND WHY YOU NEED IT

Increase your visibility

Brenda M. Spalding

Copyright©2023 Brenda M. Spalding

ISBN: 978-1-7363789-8-4

No part of this publication may be reproduced, stored in a retrieval system, transmitted in any form or by any means, electronic, mechanical, photocopying, recording or otherwise, without prior written permission of the publisher, the author or her heirs.

bradenriverconsulting@gmail.com

www.bradenriverconsulting.com

If no one knows you exist how can you sell your book?

Establishing an Author's Platform

This course provides a comprehensive guide to establishing an author's platform. Learn the importance of an author's platform, strategies for building a platform for traditional and independent publishing, utilizing social media, podcasting, engaging with the local community, targeting the right audience, and more. By the end of the course, you will have the knowledge and tools to develop a personalized author's platform plan.

Curriculum

01
Introduction to an Author's Platform
Key takeaway 🏃 Actionable step ❓ Quiz

02
Building a Platform for Traditional Publishing

03
Establishing a Platform for Independent Publishing

04
Utilizing Social Media for Author's Platform

05
Expanding the Author's Platform through Podcasting

06
Engaging with the Local Community

07
Targeting the Right Audience

08

Introduction to an Author's Platform

Overview of an author's platform and its importance

Lesson 01

An author's platform is a crucial aspect of their career and plays a significant role in their success. It can be compared to a political campaign, where candidates aim to make themselves known and gain the support of the public. Similarly, an author wants their readers to know who they are and what they stand for. The platform serves as a way to establish a connection with readers and build a loyal fan base.

Comparison of an author's platform to a political campaign

Just like a political candidate, an author needs to convey their beliefs, values, and expertise to their audience. Readers want to know who the author is, where they come from, and what credentials they have. This information helps readers understand the author's perspective and decide whether they resonate with their ideas or not. In a political campaign, candidates strive to answer the question, "What's in it for me?" Similarly, authors need to demonstrate the value readers will get from reading their book and how their expertise can enrich the readers' lives.

Understanding the need for readers to know the author and their credentials

Readers seek assurance that authors are knowledgeable and credible in their chosen subject matter. They want to know that the author has the necessary expertise and experience to write about a particular topic. Just as voters want to know that a political candidate is well-informed and capable of addressing their concerns, readers want to ensure that authors know what they are writing about. By establishing their credentials, authors can gain the trust and confidence of their readers, making them more likely to engage with their work.

Exploring the reasons why authors need a platform

Authors need a platform for several reasons, regardless of whether they are pursuing traditional publishing or self-publishing:

1. **Traditional publishing**: In the traditional publishing route, authors need to attract the attention of literary agents and publishers. Sending out query letters alone is not sufficient to secure a book deal. Agents and publishers want to see that authors have a platform that can help sell their book. By showcasing their expertise and demonstrating a readership base, authors increase their chances of getting noticed by agents and publishers.

2. **Self-publishing**: Even in self-publishing, where authors have more control over the publishing process, having a platform is crucial. Without a platform, authors may struggle to promote their book effectively and reach their target audience. Establishing an author's platform allows them to create awareness about their book, connect with readers, and generate interest and sales.

Conclusion

In conclusion, an author's platform is essential for their success in the publishing world. It serves as a means to connect with readers, showcase expertise, and build a loyal fan base. By understanding the importance of an author's platform and the parallels it shares with a political campaign, authors can effectively establish their presence, gain reader trust, and increase their chances of success in both traditional and self-publishing.

Key takeaway

An author's platform is crucial for their success in the publishing world. It allows them to connect with readers, showcase their expertise, and build a loyal fan base.

For example, a political candidate needs to convince voters by showcasing their qualifications, values, and plans. Similarly, an author needs to demonstrate their expertise, share their background, and convey the value readers will get from their book.

Actionable step

Take the first step in building your author's platform by identifying your target audience and understanding their needs and interests. This will help you tailor your content and messaging to resonate with your readers.

Quiz

What is an author's platform?

A way for authors to connect with readers and build a loyal fan base.
A type of software used by authors to write and publish their books.

Quiz

Why do readers want to know an author's credentials?

To ensure that the author is knowledgeable and credible in their chosen subject matter.
To find out if the author has won any awards.
To see if the author has a large social media following.

Quiz

What is the benefit of having an author's platform in traditional publishing?

It increases the chances of being noticed by literary agents and publishers.
It allows authors to have more control over the publishing process.
It helps authors promote their book effectively.

Lesson 02

Building a Platform for Traditional Publishing

Understanding the Role of Agents and Publishers in Traditional Publishing

In traditional publishing, agents and publishers play a crucial role in getting your book published and reaching a wider audience. It's important to understand their role and how they can help you in your publishing journey.

- Agents act as intermediaries between authors and publishers. They review and represent authors' works to publishers, negotiate contracts, and handle the business side of publishing. They are crucial in helping you secure a book deal with a reputable publishing house.

- Publishers are responsible for editing, designing, printing, and distributing your book. They have the resources and expertise to market and promote your book to a larger audience. Publishers also have established relationships with bookstores and can help get your book on shelves.

Exploring the Importance of Demonstrating Marketability and Reader Engagement

To secure a book deal with a traditional publisher, you need to demonstrate that your book has market potential and can engage readers. Publishers want to ensure that your book will sell and resonate with the target audience.

- Your author's platform plays a key role in demonstrating marketability. It shows publishers that you have a built-in audience and can effectively promote your book. This includes showcasing your online presence, social media following, and any previous writing credentials or expertise.

- Engaging readers is crucial for publishers, as they want to ensure that your book will be well-received. Your platform should communicate who you are as an author, your background, and what readers can expect from your book. This helps build trust and interest in your work.

Strategies for Showcasing Expertise and Credibility as an Author

To stand out in the competitive publishing industry, it's important to showcase your expertise and credibility as an author. This helps establish your authority and builds confidence in your writing.

- Highlight your credentials and expertise in your author's platform. If you have relevant educational background, professional experience, or specialized knowledge in the subject matter of your book, make sure to emphasize it. This shows publishers that you are knowledgeable and credible in your field.

- Consider speaking at conferences or events related to your book's subject matter. This allows you to share your expertise with a wider audience and establish yourself as an authority in your niche. It also provides networking opportunities with other authors and industry professionals.

Discussing the Shift in Responsibility for Book Promotion from Publishers to Authors

Gone are the days when publishers solely handled book promotion. Nowadays, authors are expected to actively promote their books and engage with readers. Understanding this shift in responsibility is crucial for traditional publishing success.

- Publishers now expect authors to have an active role in promoting their books. This includes using social media platforms like Facebook, X (Twitter), Instagram, and LinkedIn to connect with readers and create buzz around your book. A strong online presence can attract publishers and demonstrate your marketing potential.

- Book signings, attending events, and speaking engagements are effective ways to promote your book and connect with potential readers. These activities help build your author's platform and create opportunities for word-of-mouth marketing.

- It's important to understand that traditional bookstores may not always carry self-published books. However, by actively promoting your book and building your author's platform, you can still reach your target audience and generate sales.

Remember, building a platform for traditional publishing requires demonstrating marketability, engaging readers, showcasing expertise, and taking an active role in book promotion. By understanding the role of agents and publishers, and effectively utilizing your author's platform, you can increase your chances of securing a book deal and reaching a wider audience.

Key takeaway

Understanding the role of agents and publishers in traditional publishing is crucial for authors aspiring to secure a book deal and reach a wider audience.

For example, if an author wants to publish a book, they need to work with agents who act as intermediaries between authors and publishers. Agents review and represent authors' works to publishers, negotiate contracts, and handle the business side of publishing. Publishers, on the other hand, are responsible for editing, designing, printing, and distributing the book.

Actionable Step

Take the actionable step of researching and identifying reputable agents and publishers in your genre. Start building relationships and submitting your work to them for consideration.

Quiz

What is the role of agents in traditional publishing?

Representing authors' works to publishers
Editing and designing the book
Promoting the book to a wider audience

Quiz

What is the role of publishers in traditional publishing?

Negotiating contracts with authors
Printing and distributing the book.
Building the author's platform

Quiz

Why is it important for authors to demonstrate marketability and reader engagement?

To secure a book deal with a traditional publisher
To attract agents to represent their work
To build a strong author's platform

Quiz

How can authors showcase their expertise and credibility?

By highlighting their educational background
By attending book signings and events
By promoting their book on social media

Quiz

What is the shift in responsibility for book promotion?

From authors to publishers
From publishers to authors
From agents to authors

Lesson 03

Establishing a Platform for Independent Publishing

Exploring the Challenges Faced by Self-Published Authors

Self-publishing has become a popular option for authors who want to take control of their book's publishing process. However, self-published authors often face unique challenges that can hinder the success of their books. Let's explore some of these challenges:

1. Limited Shelf Space: Unlike traditionally published books, self-published books may not have the opportunity to be displayed on the shelves of major bookstores like Barnes and Noble. This is because big publishing houses rent space on their shelves for their authors, making it difficult for independent authors to compete for visibility.

2. Non-Returnable Books: Most bookstores prefer to sell books on a consignment basis, allowing them to return unsold books and make room for new ones. However, self-published books are often non-returnable, which can deter bookstores from carrying them. (More on this later)

Understanding the Significance of an Author's Platform in Promoting Self-Published Books

To overcome the challenges of self-publishing, establishing an author's platform becomes crucial. An author's platform refers to their online presence, reputation, and ability to reach and engage with their target readers. Let's delve into why an author's platform is significant:

1. Building Credibility: Readers want to know about the author behind the book. By having a platform, you can showcase your credentials, expertise, and background, establishing yourself as a credible author. This helps readers trust your work and increases the chances of them considering your book.

2. Connecting with Readers: An author's platform allows you to connect directly with your target readers. Through social media platforms like Facebook, Twitter, Instagram, and LinkedIn, you can engage in conversations, share updates, and build a loyal reader base. By understanding your readers' preferences and interests, you can tailor your marketing efforts to effectively reach them.

Identifying Target Readers and Reaching Out to Them Effectively

To establish an effective author's platform, it is essential to identify your target readers and reach out to them in a meaningful way. Here's how you can do it:

1. **Define Your Audience:** Consider the demographic and psychographic characteristics of your ideal readers. Are they male or female? Young or old? What are their interests and preferences? Understanding your audience will help you tailor your marketing efforts and communication style accordingly.

2. **Choose the Right Channels:** Once you know your target readers, select the social media channels that align with their preferences. For example, if your readers are more visually inclined, focus on platforms like Instagram. If they prefer concise updates, Twitter might be the right choice. Utilize these channels to share engaging content related to your book and connect with your audience.

Strategies for Promoting Self-Published Books and Increasing Visibility

Promoting self-published books requires proactive efforts from the author. Here are some strategies to consider:

1. **Book Signings and local events:** Approach local independent bookstores and offer book signings or events. Additionally, explore opportunities at assisted living centers, social clubs, and community craft fairs. These events provide a chance to connect with potential readers and create awareness about your book.

2. **Speaking Engagements:** Consider speaking at conferences or events related to your book's subject matter. Share your expertise, whether it's about editing, formatting, creating children's books, or social media marketing. By offering valuable insights, you can establish yourself as an authority in your field and attract the attention of other authors and potential readers.

3. **Collaborate with Influencers:** Identify influencers or bloggers in your genre or niche and collaborate with them. Offer them a free copy of your book for an honest review or ask if they would be interested in featuring an interview or guest post from you. Leveraging their

existing audience can significantly increase your book's visibility.

Remember, establishing an author's platform takes time and effort. Consistency and authenticity are key. By connecting with your target readers, showcasing your expertise, and actively promoting your book, you can increase its visibility and maximize its potential for success in the self-publishing world.

Key takeaway

Establishing an author's platform is crucial for self-published authors to overcome challenges and promote their books effectively.

For example, by building a strong online presence through social media platforms and engaging with target readers, authors can establish credibility and increase their book's visibility.

Actionable step

Take the time to define your target audience and choose the right social media channels to reach them. Share engaging content related to your book and actively connect with your audience.

Quiz

What are some challenges faced by self-published authors?

Limited shelf space in major bookstores
Non-returnable books
Difficulty in establishing credibility.
Lack of social media presence

Quiz

What is the significance of an author's platform?

To establish credibility and trust
To connect with target readers
To increase book sales
To avoid self-publishing challenges

Quiz

What is an actionable step to promote self-published books?

Approach local bookstores for book signings
Collaborate with influencers in your genre
Create an author's platform
Write a compelling book description

Lesson 04

Utilizing Social Media for Author's Platform

Introduction to Various Social Media Platforms

- As an author, it is important to establish a strong online presence to connect with your readers and promote your book. One effective way to do this is by utilizing various social media platforms.
- Social media platforms such as Facebook, Twitter (X), Instagram, and LinkedIn can help you reach a wider audience and engage with potential readers.
- In this lesson, we will explore how you can effectively utilize these social media platforms to build your author's platform and promote your book.

Creating a Facebook Business/Author Page

- One of the first steps in establishing your author's platform is creating a Facebook business or author page. This page will serve as a dedicated space for you to connect with your readers and promote your book.
- Unlike personal Facebook pages, a business or author page allows you to separate your personal life from your professional author's personal life.
- On your Facebook author page, you can share updates about your writing process, book release dates, and upcoming events such as book signings or speaking engagements.
- You can also share excerpts from your book, behind-the-scenes insights, and engage with your readers through comments and messages.

- By actively managing and promoting your Facebook author page, you can build a community of dedicated readers and increase your book's visibility.

Leveraging Twitter and Instagram for Book Promotion and Engagement

- In addition to Facebook, Twitter (X) and Instagram are powerful social media platforms that can help you promote your book and engage with your readers.
- On Twitter (X), you can connect with other authors, publishers, and book enthusiasts who share similar interests. By following and engaging with these individuals, you can expand your network and reach a wider audience.
- Twitter (X) is also an ideal platform to share updates about your writing process, book recommendations, and engage in conversations with your readers. You can use hashtags related to your book's genre or topic to increase visibility and attract potential readers.
- Instagram, on the other hand, is a visual platform that allows you to share images and videos related to your book. You can post aesthetically pleasing book covers, sneak peeks of your writing process, or even quotes from your book as visually appealing images.
- By using relevant hashtags and engaging with your followers, you can create a visually appealing and engaging Instagram profile that attracts potential readers and promotes your book effectively.

Utilizing LinkedIn as a Business Connection to the Local Community

- Apart from the more popular social media platforms, LinkedIn provides a unique opportunity for authors to connect with their local community and establish themselves as professionals in their field.

- As an author, you can create a LinkedIn profile that highlights your writing experience, expertise, and any relevant accomplishments. This can help you connect with other professionals in the publishing industry, local bookstores, and writing communities.

- By actively engaging with your LinkedIn connections, you can stay updated on industry trends, participate in discussions, and even find opportunities to speak at conferences or events related to your book's genre or topic.

- LinkedIn can also serve as a platform to showcase your writing skills through articles or blog posts. This can help you establish yourself as a thought leader in your niche and attract potential readers who are interested in your writing style or subject matter.

Conclusion

- In conclusion, utilizing social media platforms such as Facebook, Twitter (X), Instagram, and LinkedIn can greatly enhance your author's platform and help you promote your book effectively.

- By creating a dedicated Facebook business or author page, leveraging Twitter (X) and Instagram for book promotion and engagement, and utilizing LinkedIn as a business connection to the local community, you can connect with your readers, expand your network, and increase your book's visibility.
- Remember to tailor your content and engagement strategies to your target audience and the unique features of each social media platform. With consistent effort and thoughtful engagement, social media can become a valuable tool in building your author's platform and connecting with readers.

Key takeaway

Utilizing social media platforms such as Facebook, Twitter, Instagram, and LinkedIn can greatly enhance an author's platform and help promote their book effectively.

For example, by creating a dedicated Facebook business or author page, an author can connect with their readers, share updates about their writing process, and engage with their audience through comments and messages.

Actionable step
Create a Facebook business or author page and start sharing updates about your writing process, book release dates, and upcoming events to connect with your readers and promote your book.

Lesson 04

Expanding the Author's Platform through Podcasting

Understanding the benefits and challenges of podcasting for authors

- Podcasting is a powerful tool for authors to expand their platform and reach a wider audience.
- Unlike other social media platforms, podcasts allow for longer-form content, providing authors with the opportunity to delve deeper into their topics and engage their listeners on a more personal level.
- By hosting a podcast, authors can establish themselves as experts in their field and build credibility among their audience.
- Podcasting also offers the potential for monetization through sponsorships and advertising, providing authors with an additional source of income.
- However, it's important to note that podcasting can be challenging and time-consuming. Authors need to be prepared to invest in the necessary equipment, software, and editing skills, as well as commit to a regular podcasting schedule.

Exploring the technical aspects of starting a podcast

- To start a podcast, authors will need a few essential tools: a good quality microphone, headphones, and audio editing software.
- It is recommended to invest in a USB microphone, as it offers better sound quality and is easy to set up.
- Authors can use free audio editing software like Audacity or GarageBand to edit their podcast episodes and add music or sound effects.
- Additionally, authors will need a reliable hosting platform to upload and distribute their podcast episodes. Popular hosting platforms can be found by Googling.
- Authors should also consider creating cover art and a catchy podcast name that reflects the content and attracts potential listeners.

Strategies for creating engaging and informative podcast content

- Before diving into creating podcast episodes, authors should define their target audience and tailor their content to meet their needs and interests.
- Researching other podcasts in the same genre or niche can provide inspiration and help authors identify gaps in the market that they can fill with their unique perspective.
- It's important to plan each episode in advance, creating a structure or outline to guide the

conversation and ensure a coherent flow of information.

- Authors can invite guest speakers or experts in related fields to provide additional insights and perspectives.

- Incorporating storytelling techniques, personal anecdotes, and humor can make the podcast more engaging and relatable to the audience.

- Authors should also encourage audience interaction by inviting listeners to submit questions or topics for future episodes.

Discussing the potential impact of podcasting on an author's platform

- Hosting a podcast can significantly expand an author's platform by reaching a new and diverse audience.

- Podcasts provide an intimate and personal connection with listeners, fostering a sense of trust and loyalty towards the author.

- By consistently delivering valuable content through their podcast, authors can cultivate a dedicated following and increase their book sales and readership.

- Podcasting also opens doors for collaboration opportunities with other authors, influencers, or industry experts, further enhancing an author's visibility and reach.

- However, it's important for authors to remember that podcasting is just one piece of the puzzle. It should be integrated into a broader marketing strategy that includes social media promotion, book signings, and other offline events.

Conclusion

- Podcasting offers authors a unique opportunity to expand their platform, connect with their audience on a deeper level, and establish themselves as authorities in their field.

By understanding the benefits and challenges of podcasting, exploring the technical aspects, creating engaging content, and leveraging the potential impact, authors can harness the power of podcasting to enhance their author's platform and achieve their goals.

Key takeaway

Podcasting offers authors a unique opportunity to expand their platform, connect with their audience on a deeper level, and establish themselves as authorities in their field.

For example, an author who hosts a podcast on self-help topics can share personal stories and insights that resonate with their audience. This personal connection can help build trust and loyalty among listeners.

Actionable step

Take the first step towards starting a podcast by researching and investing in the necessary equipment and software. Create a plan for your podcast, including topics, guests, and a schedule.

Quiz

What are some benefits of podcasting for authors?

Reaching a wider audience
Establishing credibility
Opportunity for monetization
All of the above

Quiz

What are some challenges of podcasting for authors?

Time-consuming
Investment in equipment and software
Commitment to a regular schedule
All of the above

Quiz

How can authors create engaging podcast content?

Planning each episode in advance
Incorporating storytelling techniques
Inviting guest speakers
All of the above

Quiz

What is an important aspect of integrating podcasting into an author's marketing strategy?

Social media promotion
Offline events
Collaboration opportunities
All of the above

Lesson 05

Engaging with the Local Community
Exploring opportunities for book signings and author events

- As an author, it is important to engage with your local community to promote your book and connect with potential readers. One effective way to do this is by organizing book signings and author events.

- Book signings provide an opportunity for you to interact with readers, sign copies of your book, and create a personal connection with your audience.

- To find opportunities for book signings, consider reaching out to local independent bookstores. These bookstores often host author events and may be open to collaborating with you.

- Additionally, consider approaching other venues such as assisted living centers, social clubs, or community centers. These places may be interested in hosting book signings and provide a different audience for you to engage in.

- When reaching out to potential venues, highlight the benefits they will gain from hosting your event. Emphasize the opportunity for increased foot traffic and exposure for their establishment.

- Remember to tailor your pitch to each venue, considering their specific interests and target audience. For example, if your book is a children's book, approach daycare centers or schools to host a book signing.

Participating in community events, craft fairs, and book festivals

- In addition to book signings, participating in community events, craft fairs, and book festivals can be a great way to engage with your local community and promote your book.

- Look for events such as church bazaars, community craft fairs, reading festivals, and book fairs in your area. These events attract a diverse crowd and provide an opportunity for you to showcase your book.

- By participating in these events, you can interact with potential readers, share information about your book, and even sell copies directly to interested individuals.

- Networking with other vendors at these events can also lead to new opportunities and connections within the writing and publishing community. Keep your eyes and ears open for potential collaborations or future events to attend.

Offering to speak at conferences and sharing expertise with other authors

- As an author, you have unique knowledge and expertise that can benefit other authors. Offering to speak at conferences allows you to share your insights and establish yourself as an authority in your field.

- Identify conferences or events that align with your area of expertise. For example, if you are an editor or formatter, look for conferences focused on writing and publishing.

- Craft a compelling proposal highlighting the value you can bring to the conference attendees. Consider topics such as social media strategies for authors, book marketing techniques, or writing tips based on your own experience.
- By sharing your expertise, you not only contribute to the writing community but also gain exposure and credibility as an author.
- Remember to tailor your talks to the specific audience attending the conference. Consider their interests, needs, and level of experience as writers.

Conclusion

Engaging with your local community is essential for establishing your author's platform. By exploring opportunities for book signings and author events, participating in community events and festivals, and offering to speak at conferences, you can connect with potential readers, share your expertise, and promote your book effectively. Remember to tailor your approach to each audience and venue, ensuring that your message resonates with your target readership.

Key takeaway

Engaging with your local community is essential for establishing your author's platform.

By exploring opportunities for book signings and author events, participating in community events and festivals, and offering to speak at conferences, you can connect with potential readers, share your expertise, and promote your book effectively.

Actionable step
Tailor your approach to each audience and venue, ensuring that your message resonates with your target readership.

Quiz

What is one benefit of organizing book signings and author events?

Interacting with readers
Selling copies of your book
Establishing yourself as an authority in your field

Quiz

What are some venues you can approach for book signings?

Local independent bookstores
Assisted living centers
Social clubs
All of the above

Quiz

What can participating in community events and festivals help you achieve?

Interacting with potential readers
Sharing information about your book
Networking with other vendors
All of the above

Quiz

What should you consider when crafting a proposal to speak at conferences?

The value you can bring to the conference attendees
The specific interests and needs of the audience
Your own unique knowledge and expertise
All of the above

Lesson 06

Targeting the Right Audience

Understanding the importance of identifying the target audience for a book

Identifying the target audience for your book is a crucial step in establishing your author's platform. By understanding who your potential readers are, you can effectively tailor your promotional efforts and connect with the right audience. Let's explore why this is so important.

Analyzing the characteristics and preferences of potential readers

To effectively target your audience, it is essential to analyze the characteristics and preferences of potential readers. Consider the following factors:

- Demographics: Are your potential readers predominantly male or female? What is their age group? Understanding these demographics will help you tailor your messaging and communication style.

- Interests and preferences: What are the interests and preferences of your potential readers? Do they enjoy profound philosophical discussions or are they looking for a light-hearted cozy mystery for the beach? Understanding their preferences will help you align your book content with their expectations.

Tailoring promotional efforts and talks to specific audience groups.

Once you have identified your target audience and analyzed their characteristics and preferences, it's time to tailor your promotional efforts and talks to specific audience groups. Here are some strategies to consider:

- Social media presence: Create a Facebook business/author page and engage with your audience on platforms like Twitter and Instagram. Connect with individuals and communities that share similar interests and promote your book to them.

- Book signings and events: Reach out to local independent bookstores and offer to do book signings. Look for opportunities to participate in church bazaars, community craft fairs, reading festivals, and book fairs. These events allow you to directly engage with your target audience and build connections.

- Speaking engagements: Offer to speak at conferences or events related to your book's subject matter. For example, if you are an editor or formator, share your expertise in those areas. By offering valuable insights to other authors and industry professionals, you can establish yourself as an authority in your niche and attract your target audience.

Discussing the significance of aligning book content with the target audience

Aligning your book content with the preferences and expectations of your target audience is crucial for success. By understanding their needs and desires, you can deliver a book that resonates with them. Consider the following:

- Relevance and relatability: Ensure that your book addresses topics or themes that are relevant and relatable to your target audience. This will increase their interest and engagement with your book.

- Tone and style: Tailor the tone and style of your writing to match the preferences of your target audience. Whether they prefer a serious and thought-provoking tone or a light-hearted and humorous style, adapt your writing to cater to their preferences.

In conclusion, targeting the right audience for your book is essential for establishing your author's platform. By understanding the characteristics and preferences of your potential readers, tailoring your promotional efforts, and aligning your book content with their expectations, you can effectively connect with your target audience and increase the chances of success for your book.

Key takeaway

Identifying the target audience for your book is a crucial step in establishing your author's platform.

For example, if you are writing a self-help book for young adults, your target audience would be individuals between the ages of 18-30 who are looking for personal growth and development.

Actionable step

Take some time to research and analyze the characteristics and preferences of your potential readers. This will help you understand who your target audience is and how to effectively connect with them.

Quiz

Why is it important to identify the target audience for your book?

To tailor your promotional efforts and connect with the right audience.
To increase your chances of success as an author.
To establish yourself as an authority in your niche.

Quiz

What are some strategies for tailoring promotional efforts to specific audience groups?

Creating a social media presence and engaging with your audience.
Offering to speak at conferences or events related to your book's subject matter.
Reaching out to local independent bookstores for book signings.

Quiz

Why is it important to align your book content with the preferences and expectations of your target audience?

To increase their interest and engagement with your book.
To establish yourself as an authority in your niche.
To tailor your promotional efforts and connect with the right audience.

Lesson 07

Review and Application

Reviewing Key Concepts and Strategies

In this lesson, we will review the key concepts and strategies covered throughout the course on establishing an author's platform. By understanding these concepts and strategies, you will be better equipped to develop a personalized author's platform plan.

The Importance of an Author's Platform

- An author's platform is crucial for connecting with readers and promoting your book.
- It is similar to a political campaign, where the candidate wants people to get to know them and understand their values and qualifications.
- Readers want to know who you are, where you come from, and what credentials you have as an author.
- Building a platform helps establish credibility and trust with readers, making them more likely to be interested in your book.

Establishing an Author's Platform

1. Social Media Presence

    - Create a dedicated Facebook business/author page to engage with readers and promote your book.
    - Utilize Twitter to connect with like-minded individuals and share updates about your book.

- Use Instagram to showcase visuals related to your book and engage with your audience.
- LinkedIn can be used to establish professional connections within the local community.

2. Podcasting

    - Consider starting a podcast, as it can be a powerful tool for reaching a wider audience.
    - Although it may require technical expertise, podcasting can yield significant results in terms of promoting your book and establishing yourself as an authority in your field.

3. Getting Out and About

    - Offer to do book signings at local independent bookstores to connect with potential readers.
    - Explore opportunities to speak at conferences or events related to your book's subject matter.
    - Attend church bazaars, community craft fairs, reading festivals, and book fairs to network with other vendors and reach a broader audience.

4. Identifying Your Audience

    - Determine who your target audience is based on factors such as age, gender, and interests.
    - Tailor your marketing efforts and speaking engagements to appeal to your specific audience.

- Understand the preferences and expectations of your audience to effectively promote and sell your book.

Applying the Knowledge Gained

Now that we have reviewed the key concepts and strategies, it's time to apply this knowledge and develop a personalized author's platform plan. Consider the following steps:

1. Identify Your Goals

    - Determine what you want to achieve with your author's platform. Is it to increase book sales, establish yourself as an expert, or connect with a specific audience?
    - Clearly define your goals to guide your platform development.

2. Assess Your Resources

    - Evaluate the resources you have available to build your platform, such as time, budget, and technical skills.
    - Identify areas where you may need additional support or resources.

3. Choose Appropriate Platforms

    - Based on your target audience and goals, select the social media platforms and marketing channels that are most likely to reach and engage your audience effectively.

- Consider the platforms discussed earlier, such as Facebook, Twitter, Instagram, LinkedIn, and podcasting.

4. Developing a Content Strategy

    - Create a plan for regularly producing and sharing content that aligns with your book's themes and appeals to your target audience.
    - Determine the types of content that will resonate with your audience, such as blog posts, videos, or podcast episodes.

5. Implement and Monitor

    - Start implementing your author's platform plan by consistently engaging with your audience on social media, attending events, and leveraging other marketing strategies.
    - Monitor the performance of your efforts and adjust your strategy as needed based on audience feedback and analytics.

Discussing Potential Challenges and Solutions

Implementing an author's platform plan can come with its own set of challenges. Let's discuss some common challenges and potential solutions:

1. Time Constraints

- As an author, you may already have limited time available for writing. Balancing platform development with writing can be challenging.
- Solution: Prioritize and schedule specific time slots for platform-related activities, ensuring you allocate time for both writing and platform building.

2. Technical Expertise

- Podcasting and utilizing certain social media platforms may require technical skills that you may not possess.
- Solution: Consider seeking assistance from professionals or taking online courses to develop the necessary skills or outsource certain tasks.

3. Reaching the Right Audience

- Identifying and reaching your target audience can be difficult, especially if you are unsure of their preferences and where to find them.
- Solution: Conduct market research to better understand your audience's demographics, interests, and preferred platforms. Utilize targeted advertising and collaborations with influencers to reach your desired audience.

Q&A Session and Final Thoughts

In this final part of the lesson, we will open the floor for a Q&A session. You can ask any remaining questions you have regarding establishing an effective author's platform. We will also share some final thoughts on the importance of ongoing platform development and the potential impact it can have on your book's success.

Remember, an author's platform is not a one-time effort but an ongoing process. It requires consistent engagement, adaptation to new trends, and continuous promotion to build a loyal readership and increase book sales.

Thank you for participating in this course on establishing an author's platform. We hope you found it informative and empowering. Good luck in your journey as an author!

Key takeaway

Establishing an author's platform is crucial for connecting with readers, promoting your book, and establishing credibility and trust.

For example, by creating a dedicated Facebook page, engaging with readers on social media, and attending book signings and events, you can build a platform that allows you to connect with your audience and promote your book effectively.

Actionable step

Develop a personalized author's platform plan by identifying your goals, assessing your resources, choosing appropriate platforms, developing a content strategy, and implementing and monitoring your efforts.

Quiz

Why is establishing an author's platform important?

To connect with readers and promote your book
To establish yourself as an expert
To increase book sales
All of the above

Quiz

What is one strategy for establishing an author's platform?

Creating a dedicated Facebook page
Attending book signings
Engaging with readers on social media
All of the above

Quiz

What is an actionable step for developing an author's platform?

Identifying your goals
Assessing your resources
Choosing appropriate platforms
All of the above

Lesson 08

Nice! You've just completed *Establishing an Author's Platform.*

Here's a recap of what you've learned:

- An author's platform is crucial for their success in the publishing world. It allows them to connect with readers, showcase their expertise, and build a loyal fan base.
- Understanding the role of agents and publishers in traditional publishing is crucial for authors aspiring to secure a book deal and reach a wider audience.
- Establishing an author's platform is crucial for self-published authors to overcome challenges and promote their books effectively.
- Utilizing social media platforms such as Facebook, Twitter, Instagram, and LinkedIn can greatly enhance an author's platform and help promote their book effectively.
- Podcasting offers authors a unique opportunity to expand their platform, connect with their audience on a deeper level, and establish themselves as authorities in their field.
- Engaging with your local community is essential for establishing your author's platform.

- Identifying the target audience for your book is a crucial step in establishing your author's platform.
- Establishing an author's platform is crucial for connecting with readers, promoting your book, and establishing credibility and trust.

My thoughts on independent publishing.

I have self-published over 29 of my own books and several more for other authors.

A cautionary tale when you are looking for someone to do all the heavy work for you. **Do your research.**

Do not give thousands of dollars to a company on the internet before you know what you are getting.

After you have written your masterpiece and gone over it countless times and are ready to let it fly, have it edited by an independent eye. Not the retired high school English teacher next door for free or a friend of a friend for very little that says they can do it over the weekend.

Pay a professional editor. There are different types of editors.

With Developmental editing, you can expect

- Developmental edit - A detailed editorial letter with an analysis of your manuscript and specific revision suggestions
- An annotated copy of your manuscript containing specific notes and edits

With copy editing, you can expect:

- A thoroughly annotated version of your manuscript with tracked changes to easily identify edits
- A style sheet listing standard spellings and formatting, which can later be referenced by your proofreader

With proofreading, you can expect:

- A final manuscript that has been meticulously proofread and corrected to the best of the proofreader's ability

Go to https://reedsy.com/editing for more information

If you are truly an Indi author you might decide to upload your book yourself. It's not that difficult.

I use either Kindle Direct Publishing which is part of Amazon or Ingram Spark.

The pros and cons

KDP

Free upload, free ISBN, KDP owns the imprint, free kindle at the same time. It's posted on Amazon. They do several sizes and make a hard cover. You can also have an AI generated audio book. Book promotion possibilities.

In taking a free ISBN there is no returnability and it is less likely that even independent bookstores will shelve your book.

Amazon is **a retailer**

Ingram Spark

Upload is free now for book and eBook at the same time. eBook must be in epub format. They do offer a free ISBN, but they own the imprint.

Bookstores will take the book because there is returnability.

Your book will appear on Amazon and other internet sites, Barnes and Noble etc..

Ingram Spark in part of Ingram. The largest book **distributor** in the world.

You can buy your own ISBN for $125 from Bowker. You can purchase a block of ten for $225 if you plan to write more books.

Cover presentation

A good cover will help to sell your book.

You can hire a cover designer. Design one using AI, which I have done with ChatGPT. Canva is another choice.

It's another place where you do not want to skimp and pay Suzi in high school next door to make your cover.

Being an author is more than just writing the darn book and hoping someone will buy it and enjoy it as much as you enjoyed writing it.

There is a business behind the whole thing that I find challenging. It challenges my mind to come up with a story that I hope my readers will like. It challenges me to get my butt out there and meet my readers when I'd rather stay in bed.

Pricing

We all want to make money from our books. Be careful you don't price yourself out of a sale.

A children's picture book with 30 pages will sell at $10 but may not sell at $15.

Would you rather sell ten books at $10 or two books at $15.

The same goes for novels. Don't price yourself out of a sale.

It's a journey

If you are not enjoying the journey sit back and figure out where the problem is. Often joining a writer's group and talking with other writers and authors can help you solve problems.

Other authors are on the same journey that you are on. Some are father along and can help you. A writer's group can be a great resource. They are there and willing to help.

About the Author

Brenda Spalding is a talented writer who has received several awards. Her expertise in publishing and marketing makes her a regular guest speaker at writers' conferences and writers' groups.

The author is a past president of the National League of American Pen Women- Sarasota Branch, a member of the Sarasota Fiction Writers, Florida Authors and Publishers Association, and the Florida Writers Association, and on the board of directors for the Florida Writers Foundation.

The author is currently an advisor for the not-for-profit *ICreate* in Sarasota.

Her company, Braden River Consulting LLC, was formed to help other authors on their creative journey.

www.bradenriverconsulting.com
www.brendamspaldingauthor.com

www.ingramcontent.com/pod-product-compliance
Lightning Source LLC
Chambersburg PA
CBHW040003110526
44587CB00001BA/33